Ha...

LON

CW00429967

GHOST STORIES

Compiled by Julia Skinner

THE FRANCIS FRITH COLLECTION

www.francisfrith.com

First published in the United Kingdom in 2013 by The Francis Frith Collection®

This edition published exclusively for Bradwell Books in 2013
For trade enquiries see: www.bradwellbooks.com or tel: 0800 834 920
ISBN 978-1-84589-723-9

British Library Cataloguing in Publication Data

Haunted London - Ghost Stories
Compiled by Julia Skinner

The Francis Frith Collection
Oakley Business Park,
Wylye Road, Dinton,
Wiltshire SP3 5EU
Tel: +44 (0) 1722 716 376
Email: info@francisfrith.co.uk
www.francisfrith.com

Printed and bound in Malaysia
Contains material sourced from responsibly managed forests

Front Cover: **LONDON, WESTMINSTER BRIDGE c1900** L130303t
Frontispiece: **LONDON, TOWER BRIDGE 1895** L130168
Contents: **LONDON, ST PAUL'S CATHEDRAL c1860** L130282

The colour-tinting is for illustrative purposes only, and is not intended to be historically accurate

CONTENTS

Haunted
LONDON
GHOST STORIES

HAUNTED LONDON

One of the most famous buildings in the city is the historic castle
on the north bank of the River Thames known as the Tower of
London, although this is actually a complex of several buildings and
21 different towers that were erected at various periods down the
centuries, ringed by two sets of defensive walls. The oldest part of
the Tower of London complex is the building known as the White
Tower, which King William I, 'the Conqueror', had built shortly after
the Norman Conquest of England in 1066; it is the structure (with
later ogee-roofed corner turrets) in the centre of the photograph on
the opposite page, which still dominates the scene. This formidable
fortress was completed in 1078, built to dominate London and
protect the king and his family in times of disorder. Many other
buildings have been added to the Tower of London over the centuries
and it has fulfilled a variety of roles besides that of a royal residence
(that function ceased in the 17th century), including use as an arsenal,
the home of the royal menagerie, the place of safe-keeping for the
Crown Jewels and, most famously, as a notorious prison.

The Tower of London has a dark history, and countless terrible and
tragic events have taken place there over the centuries. Prisoners
of State were confined in this ancient fortress, where some were
tortured, and many only left the Tower to go to their execution.
Murders have taken place there as well as suicides and tragic deaths,
so it is not surprising that a number of unhappy shades are said to
haunt the fortress, which is reputed to be one of the most haunted
buildings in Britain. Over the centuries there have been many well-
attested ghost sightings at the Tower, and strange incidents of
mysterious phenomena there continue to be reported to the present
day. On the next few pages are some of the most famous ghost
stories linked with this iconic landmark of London.

LONDON, THE TOWER OF LONDON c1900 L130269

In the 16th and 17th centuries the basement of the White Tower housed a rack, a vicious instrument of torture, it is said by those with ears to hear that the ghostly sounds of agonized screams and cries from its unfortunate victims still echo from the tower on occasions. A spectral woman known as the White Lady is said to roam the White Tower and has been seen waving from an upper window, but who she is and why she wanders the building remains a mystery. Perhaps she is linked with the unexplained scent of perfume in the Norman chapel of St John the Evangelist on an upper floor of the building that has been reported by some people, including a custody guard on night patrol in the tower; the scent is only discernable after midnight and grows stronger throughout the night until it becomes quite overpowering, but then fades away completely by dawn.

A famous ghost story from the Tower of London is linked with King Henry VI, who reigned in the 15th century during the Wars of the Roses between two rival royal factions claiming the throne, the Houses of Lancaster and York. Following the Yorkist victory at the Battle of Tewkesbury in 1471, King Edward IV reclaimed the throne he had previously won and lost and had the Lancastrian King Henry imprisoned in the Tower, where he died 'in the hour before midnight' on 21st May 1471. He was reported to have died of melancholy, but it was widely believed that King Edward had him murdered. A plaque on the floor of the chapel in the upper chamber of the Wakefield Tower marks the spot where he is traditionally supposed to have been stabbed to death as he knelt in prayer. The pale wraith of the king is said to appear in the chapel between 11pm and midnight on the anniversary of his death; it roams fretfully around the room before disappearing into the stone walls at midnight.

One of the most notorious events linked with the Tower of London is the mysterious disappearance of the 'Princes in the Tower', 12-year-old King Edward V and 10-year-old Richard, Duke of York, the two sons of King Edward IV who were kept prisoner there by their uncle Richard, Duke of Gloucester, after he usurped the throne as King Richard III following the death of their father. King Richard is believed to have ordered the princes to be murdered in the Tower in 1483, and in 1674, during the reign of King Charles II, the skeletons of two children were discovered buried at the foot of a stairway of the White Tower – it is not known for sure if these were the remains of the princes, but King Charles believed them to be so, and they were given a royal burial in Westminster Abbey. The spirits of the tragic princes are said to haunt the White Tower and also the Bloody Tower of the castle complex, where they were lodged and are presumed to have met their deaths – sightings have been reported of two young boys clad in white nightgowns, sometimes seen walking hand in hand, and at other times as shadowy figures gliding down the stairs. The upper chamber of the Bloody Tower now houses a display about the disappearance of the two princes.

The lower chamber of the Bloody Tower is known as Raleigh's Study and is furnished as it might have appeared when Sir Walter Raleigh was imprisoned there for nearly 13 years in the early 17th century. This famous seaman, soldier, courtier, author and adventurer was a favourite of Queen Elizabeth I (1558-1693) but fell foul of her successor, King James I (1603-1625). In 1603 he was accused of plotting against the king, tried and found guilty of treason, but his death sentence was commuted to imprisonment and he was incarcerated in a small cell in the Bloody Tower until 1616. During his confinement Sir Walter was not as restricted in his movements as other prisoners kept at the Tower, and for exercise was allowed to pace along the stretch of battlemented rampart adjoining the Bloody Tower, an area now known as Raleigh's Walk. In 1616 King James I allowed Raleigh to be released so he could lead a gold-seeking expedition to South America, but a clash there with Spanish forces provoked an international incident. King James invoked Raleigh's suspended death sentence in order to appease Spain, and he was beheaded at Old Palace Yard, Westminster in 1618. It is said that Raleigh ghost haunts the rooms of the Bloody Tower where he spent his long years of captivity, and on moonlit nights you may see his restless shade traversing Raleigh's Walk where he so often strolled in his earthly life. Raleigh's ghost is also said to haunt the gatehouse of the castle complex known as the Byward Tower. On two separate occasions in the 1980s, Yeomen Warders on night watch in the Byward Tower reported seeing a mysterious figure looking in at them from the doorway of the guardroom, which then vanished into thin air after a few seconds; they both identified the figure as Raleigh, recognising it from the portrait of him that hangs in his former study in the Bloody Tower.

Another restless shade may also roam the Bloody Tower. In 1970 a female visitor saw a long-haired lady standing by a window inside the tower, dressed in a full-length black gown with a white cap on her head, and wearing a large gold medallion hung around her neck; as she watched, the figure faded away and disappeared.

The disembodied footsteps of a phantom patrol of soldiers tramping along its round from the Bloody Tower to the water-gate entrance into the Tower complex from the Thames known as Traitors' Gate have also been heard by many soldiers on guard duty at the Tower of London over the years – the sharp crack of the studs of their hobnailed boots on the roadway is clearly heard, but nothing is ever seen.

The Traitors' Gate was so named because it was through this watergate that prisoners accused of treason passed into the Tower after being brought along the river by barge. Most executions of those found guilty of their alleged crime took place either on Tower Hill, just outside the fortress, or at Tyburn on the other side of the city, but Tower Green in the precincts of the Tower itself is where two of the six wives of King Henry VIII met their deaths – Anne Boleyn in 1536 and Katherine Howard in 1542. Anne Boleyn was beheaded with a sword, rather than a headsman's axe, after being found guilty of treason and adultery on dubious grounds so King Henry could marry his third wife, Jane Seymour. Her ghost is said to roam several places around the Tower including the Chapel Royal of St Peter ad Vincula, where her remains were interred beneath the floor in an arrow box after her execution and still remain today. The white form of a headless woman that has been seen drifting across the grass of Tower Green has also been interpreted as her unhappy wraith.

KING HENRY VIII (1509-1547)

In 1541 King Henry VIII also ordered the execution of Lady Margaret Pole, Countess of Salisbury, on Tower Green. This was an act of vindictiveness against her son, Cardinal Reginald Pole, who had published a treatise denouncing King Henry's religious changes in which he had broken with the Church of Rome and made himself Head of the Church in England. King Henry was incensed by this but the Cardinal was overseas and safely out of reach, so he took his revenge on the Cardinal's elderly mother instead. He had the harmless old lady arrested, tried on a trumped-up charge of treason and imprisoned in the Tower until her execution on 27th May 1541. The Countess was brought to the scaffold kicking and screaming, and protested her innocence to the end – she refused to kneel and lay her head on the block, stoutly asserting 'So should traitors do, and I am none'. She challenged the masked axeman to remove her head 'as best he could', and he had to chase her around the scaffold, hacking at her until she collapsed from her wounds and he finally managed to behead her. A spectral re-enactment of the ghastly event is said to sometimes takes place on the anniversary of her execution.

Lady Jane Grey also met her death on Tower Green. This tragic teenage girl, known to history as 'The Nine Days' Queen', was the granddaughter of King Henry VIII's sister Mary. She was set up as a puppet queen by her father-in-law John Dudley, Duke of Northumberland, as a Protestant claimant to the throne after the death in 1553 of King Henry VIII's son King Edward VI, in preference to the true successor, the Roman Catholic Princess Mary, King Henry's daughter by his first wife, Katharine of Aragon. Northumberland's coup was unsuccessful and nine days later Mary took her rightful place on the throne as Queen Mary I. She had Lady Jane imprisoned in the Tower, where she was executed on 12th February 1554. Lady Jane Grey's ghost is also said to return occasionally to the Tower on the anniversary of her execution. A famous sighting was at 3 o'clock in the morning of 12th February 1957, when a guard on night duty at the fortress reported seeing a 'white shapeless form' silhouetted above him on the battlements of the Salt Tower.

One of the most haunted buildings of the Tower of London is the black-and-white timber-framed building on the south-west corner of Tower Green that is currently called The Queen's House (its name changes according to the sex of the reigning monarch); this was originally the home of the Lieutenant of the Tower and is now the official residence of the Governor of the Tower. (It is not open to the public.) The most famous ghost of The Queen's House is the mysterious Grey Lady in Tudor dress which can only be seen by women, but no one knows whose restless shade she is. The strange figure of a man in medieval clothes has also been seen gliding along an upper corridor of the house, and the sound of heavy footsteps has been heard on a stairway at the rear of the building, although nobody – in either earthly or spirit form – is ever seen there at the time. In 1978 a guest staying in the house also heard the unexplained sound of 'religious chanting' in the middle of the night, and when she mentioned it she was told that other guests at the house had also heard the unearthly sound, but no one knew where it was coming from.

The Queen's House is also reputed to be haunted by the spectre of Arbella Stuart, who was imprisoned in the building in 1611 and died there in 1615. This unhappy lady was a cousin of King James I (1603-1625) and therefore a claimant to the throne; she committed the great sin of marrying William Seymour (also of royal blood) without the king's permission, and this union of two possible claimants to the throne was regarded as a threat by the king. Arbella was put under house arrest and William was sent to the Tower, but his spirited wife escaped from her place of confinement and plotted to get William out of the Tower so they could flee to France. He was successfully smuggled out of the fortress but missed his rendezvous with his wife, and Arbella had to sail to France alone, leaving William to follow later. He eventually made it to France and safety, but unfortunately Arbella was recognised at Calais and sent back to England. This time she herself was sent to the Tower and she remained imprisoned there for the rest of her life, and never saw William again. She became deeply depressed and died in the Lennox Room of The Queen's House in 1615. There were rumours at the time of her death that she had been murdered, perhaps poisoned, but modern scholars believe this unhappy lady actually starved herself to death in despair at her fate, so it is not surprising that her sad shade haunts the room where she breathed her last. It is noticeably colder than the other rooms in the house with a strange, forbidding atmosphere, and a peculiar odour lingers in the air. Several women who have slept in the room have woken up in terror, convinced they were about to be suffocated. The section about the ghosts of the Tower of London on the Historic Royal Palaces website (www.hrp.org.uk) tells how the Governor of the Tower from 1994-2006 (Major General Geoffrey Field) and his wife were so convinced the Lennox Room was haunted that they never allowed unaccompanied female guests to sleep there.

After its long, dark history, the Tower of London has now entered a phase of glorious retirement as a museum and tourist attraction, but a poignant reminder of its past is the modern memorial on Tower Green commemorating all those who were executed there by order of the State. Around it is a poem composed by the artist, Brian Catling, which relates equally well to all the people who suffered and died in this historic but notorious place over the centuries: 'Gentle visitor pause awhile: where you stand death cut away the light of many days: here jewelled names were broken from the vivid thread of life: may they rest in peace while we walk the generations around their strife and courage: under these restless skies'. Sadly, it seems from the many ghost stories linked with the Tower of London that not all of them have managed to 'rest in peace'.

LONDON, TOWER BRIDGE UNDER CONSTRUCTION 1890 L130050

Spanning the River Thames near the Tower of London is the iconic
Tower Bridge. The first stone for the bridge was laid in 1886, and it
was officially opened in 1894. The bridge is seen in all its glory in
the photograph on the title page of this book, and is shown here in
skeletal state whilst under construction in 1890, before its interior
metal framework was encased in stone. Tower Bridge is a combined
suspension and lifting bridge, and its bascules carrying the roadway
can be fully raised to allow tall-masted ships and sailing barges to
pass through. The hydraulic machinery that raises the heavy bascules
was originally driven by steam, but was converted to an electric-
hydraulic drive system in 1974. When the bridge was constructed the
upper deck linking its two towers formed walkways so pedestrians
could still cross the Thames when the bascules were raised.
Nowadays the walkways form part of the Tower Bridge Exhibition
about the bridge's history and construction, which is housed in its
twin towers, the high-level walkways and the Victorian Engine Rooms
on the south side of the bridge, where visitors can see some of the
original hydraulic machinery and steam engines.

There were a number of deaths during construction work on the bridge between 1886 and 1894 – between 5 and 10 workmen died there, according to various sources of information – and over the years a sad number of people have committed suicide by jumping from the bridge into the river. A little known fact about the bridge is that the tower on the north bank of the Thames near the Tower of London holds a dark secret – a small room in its base used to be a mortuary, known as 'Dead Man's Hole', where the corpses of people found in the Thames (either through suicide, murder or accident) were taken after retrieval from the river and stored there until claimed by relatives and taken away for burial. The corpses were brought along the Thames by boat, and the base of the tower formed a landing platform with a set of stairs to the morgue.

Given all the above, it is not surprising that a number of restless shades are said to linger around Tower Bridge. Some people have reported seeing ghostly shadows on the upper walkways, and others have felt their clothes being tugged by an unseen hand. Tower Bridge was investigated in an episode of the TV series 'Most Haunted Live' which aired in October 2005, featuring the medium Derek Acorah. He reported sensing three unquiet spirits around him on the walkways of the bridge, one of which he felt was the shade of a man who had drowned himself, and another member of the team heard strange noises on the walkway that no one could explain. When the team moved to the former Bridge Master's Quarters (now a suite of rooms used for private functions) the dog accompanying them appeared distressed by something unseen, questions asked by the team seemed to prompt rapping noises in response, and Derek Acorah claimed to sense the presence there of a man called 'Tom'. The team then investigated Dead Man's Hole (which is not open to the public), where Derek Acorah picked up a great deal of paranormal energies that he described as like a swarm of bees, which he interpreted as angry spirits. Other paranormal investigators at Tower Bridge have also claimed to have felt the spirit presence of a disturbed, angry man in the Victorian Engine Rooms.

LONDON, LONDON BRIDGE 1890 L130034

Until the mid 18th century London Bridge was the only bridge in the city that spanned the Thames, connecting the City of London on the north side and Southwark on the south. The present London Bridge opened to traffic in 1973, and is the latest in a succession of bridges to claim the name since the first timber bridge was built by the Roman founders of London in the first century AD. The London Bridge seen in this photograph was built between 1827 and 1831, replacing the medieval one of nursery rhyme fame which had lasted for over six centuries; it was sited about 30 metres (98 feet) west of the alignment of the old medieval bridge. Demolished in 1968 and replaced by the current bridge, the London Bridge seen here was re-erected in the USA at Lake Huvasu City in Arizona in 1970.

The story of the various London Bridges in the city's history is told at the visitor attraction 'The London Bridge Experience and London Tombs', which opened in 2008 on the south bank of the Thames, immediately outside London Bridge Station. It is housed in the vaults below the southern abutment of the modern bridge. 'The London Bridge Experience' is an exhibition about the history of the bridge, whilst the 'London Tombs' is more of a popular 'scare attraction'. The 'London Tombs' was built in the remains of a former 'plague pit' (where plague victims were buried many centuries ago) and what may have been the site of an old cemetery for St Saviour's Church (now Southwark Cathedral), and although the attraction was designed to be creepily entertaining, there does seem to be something genuinely spooky about the site… On 31st October 2007 (Halloween, appropriately!) the BBC ran a story about the strange events that had taken place whilst the attraction was being constructed. When construction workers excavated the site they discovered a sealed vault containing a number of skeletons. It seems that the spirits of those people who had long ago passed over were unhappy about their remains being disturbed, as the workmen experienced a succession of uncanny events. Light bulbs on the construction site would frequently blow even though the electricians reported that everything was in perfect working order, and tools of all shapes and sizes mysteriously disappeared on a regular basis. The workmen had a definite sense of being watched, and many felt so uneasy in the eerie atmosphere of the site and apprehensive about what might be lurking there that they refused to work alone.

The strange goings-on seem to have continued since the attraction opened, with reports of poltergeist activity, the sounds of running footsteps or children's voices when no one is there, and mysterious dark shapes glimpsed in the shadows of the corridors. If you have strong nerves, you can go on an overnight paranormal investigation at the London Bridge Experience and London Tombs, but be warned – the area beneath London Bridge seems to be a very haunted place with an overpowering atmosphere of terror and gloom, and many people who have ventured there on 'ghost hunts' have been overwhelmed by a sense of sheer panic, despair and desolation…

The traditional ends of the medieval London Bridge were marked by the church of St Magnus-the-Martyr in Lower Thames Street, on the north bank of the Thames, and what is now Southwark Cathedral, on the south. In past centuries the severed heads of executed traitors were dipped in tar to preserve them against the elements and displayed on spikes on the southern gatehouse of the old bridge, as a warning to others. The custom began in 1305, when the first head displayed on the gate was that of William Wallace, the Scottish freedom fighter better known to modern filmgoers as 'Braveheart', and continued until 1660 when King Charles II put a stop to the practice. The gruesome display was one of the most notorious sights of London in the past – in 1598 a German visitor to London called Paul Hentzner recorded that he had counted over 30 heads there. Perhaps the souls of those executed victims are responsible for the mysterious sound of ghostly wailing and crying that has been reported from the former area of the medieval bridge, where the tidal River Thames flows past the church of St Magnus-the-Martyr (which also has its own tale of haunted goings-on – see opposite). However, another interpretation is that it is the spectral wailing of a group of Jews who drowned there as they were trying to leave the country in the late 13th century, after King Edward I ordered the expulsion of all Jews from England. One story about their sad end is that their ship sank at that spot, but another is that the ship they had hired to take them abroad was caught by an ebb tide and beached there on the river sands; the captain ordered everyone to leave the ship and wait on a nearby sandbank for the tide to turn, but when this happened the captain and his crew raced back to the ship and sailed away, callously leaving their helpless passengers to drown in the rising waters of the Thames.

Hidden amongst tall buildings on the north bank of the Thames near London Bridge is the church of St Magnus-the-Martyr in Lower Thames Street. The church is of very ancient foundation, but the original medieval church of St Magnus was destroyed in the Great Fire of London of 1666 and the present church is one of many London churches rebuilt to a design by Sir Christopher Wren after the fire. One of the rectors of the medieval church was Miles Coverdale (1487-1569), famous for instigating the first complete printed edition of an English translation of the Bible in 1535, who was rector of the church for two years towards the end of his life, from 1564 to 1566. After his death in 1569 he was buried at the church of St Bartholomew-by-the-Exchange in Bartholomew Lane, off Threadneedle Street, in the City of London, but when that church was demolished in 1840 his remains were moved to St Magnus and now lie in the south-east corner of the church, where there are two memorials to him. Some people think that Coverdale's ghost may be the mysterious cowled figure dressed in a clerical robe or cassock that has been seen on a number of occasions, sometimes standing in silent contemplation near his grave, and at other times appearing in various parts of the church, including the vestry and the stairs. The figure always vanishes away when it is approached, sometimes disappearing through solid walls of the church. Sightings of the strange figure have been reported by a number of reputable witnesses over the years, including a church worker, a verger, a rector's wife and the Reverend Henry Joy Fynes-Clinton, rector of the church from 1921 to 1959, who told Peter Underwood, President of the Ghost Club from 1960 to 1993 and author of many books on the paranormal, that he had 'no doubt whatever but that the church was haunted by a robed figure' and that he thought it might be the ghost of a former priest at St Magnus, if not of Coverdale himself. (Quoted in 'Haunted London' by Peter Underwood, first published in 1973.)

Another haunted church in this part of the city is that of St James Garlickhythe in Garlick Hill, between Queen Victoria Street and the Upper Thames Street dual-carriageway near Southwark Bridge, which was also rebuilt after its medieval predecessor was destroyed in the Great Fire of London. In the mid 19th century workmen clearing out a vault in the church unearthed a casket containing the embalmed and mummified corpse of a man. It used to be thought that he was a young man who died in the late 18th century, but scientific research in 2004 concluded he was an elderly man who died between 1641 and 1801. There are many theories about who he was, ranging from an early Mayor of London to a sailor who died on board a ship making for London, whose body was pickled or embalmed and then brought to the church for burial when the ship docked. For some time the grisly remains were on display in a glass case in the entrance porch of the church, accompanied with a notice giving a warning of their own mortality to the church's parishioners, who had affectionately nicknamed the corpse 'Jimmy Garlick':

> *'Stop Stranger As You Pass By.*
> *As You Are Now So once Was I.*
> *As I Am Now So Shall You Be.*
> *So Pray Prepare To Follow Me.'*

At one time the mischievous choir boys of the church would take Jimmy out of his case on Sunday mornings and sit him on a pew to listen to the service! Although this did not appear to bother his spirit, it was another story when a bomb hit the church during the Second World War, shattering the glass of his case. His disturbed shade is said to have haunted the church ever since, even though his mortal remains are now kept with more reverence in a special case in an upper room of the church tower, and are no longer open to public view. Several visitors to the church have reported seeing a shrouded ghost standing on the tower steps and in various parts of the church, and his shade may also be responsible for objects being mysteriously moved around, as well as the unexplained noises that have been heard in the building.

On the south bank of the Thames between Southwark Bridge and the London Millennium Footbridge is the Anchor pub at 34 Park Street on Bankside, an atmospheric London tavern that is home to an unusual four-legged ghost. In former times the pub was the haunt of smugglers and sailors from London's wharves and docks, making it a prime target for visits by the infamous press gang. The main method of recruitment for the Royal Navy in the Georgian period, and especially during the Napoleonic Wars, was impressment – the summary seizing of men between the ages of 18 and 55 by press gangs stationed around the coast, regardless whether they were willing to serve in the Navy or not. It might be years before a man seized by the press gang came home again – if ever – and his family could be left in poverty. It is not surprising that men targeted by the press gang would fight desperately to resist impressment, and legend says the Anchor is haunted by the ghost of a faithful dog that tried to defend his owner against just such a fate. The story goes that the press gang burst into the Anchor one night and seized the man as he was having a drink with friends. His brave dog barked and snapped at the gang as they dragged his master away, until one of them slammed the pub door shut behind them with such force that the dog's tail was trapped and completely cut off. The poor dog howled in pain and ran off, never to be seen again. However, the unfortunate hound is said to return to the Anchor in spirit form around midnight on some dark nights, and the sound of its ghostly paws can be heard padding around the pub as it searches for the rest of its tail!

Still in Southwark, the photograph on the opposite page shows the galleried George Inn at 77 Borough High Street as it looked in the 1870s, with its now-lost archway to the High Street. The George Inn was shown on a map of 1542, but an inn probably stood here long before that. The old inn burned down in 1676 but was rebuilt in the same style and remained unchanged until the late 19th century when part of it was torn down to make room for offices and warehousing for the Great Northern Railway. Borough High Street used to be lined with inns like this for stagecoach passengers, but the coaching trade was killed off by the railways in the 19th century, resulting in their demolition. What remains of the George is London's only surviving galleried inn; beautifully restored, it is now in the care of the National Trust although it still functions as a pub. This historic inn is reputedly roamed by the shade of a ghostly woman, possibly of a former landlady called Miss Agnes Murray who died in 1934. Miss Murray loved the Dickensian atmosphere of the building, and during her tenure there she stubbornly refused to modernise the inn to suit the changing times. It is said that her dislike of the modern age causes her spirit to play havoc with the electronic technology that is an essential part of the present-day inn, and her ghostly influence is blamed for problems that seem occur there with abnormal frequency, such as tills breaking down and computers crashing. Cameras also often malfunction when visitors try to take a photograph of the atmospheric interior of the building. Mysterious images that cannot be easily explained away have also been picked up by security cameras, and apparently some members of staff 'living in' at the George over the years have reported seeing a 'misty form' in their bedrooms.

LONDON, THE GEORGE INN, SOUTHWARK c1875 L130130

Someone who may well have frequented the George Inn in the past was William Shakespeare (1564-1616) who lived at Southwark for a while to be near the open-air Globe Theatre that was built in the early 17th century for his company, the Lord Chamberlain's Men. Now you can watch Shakespeare's plays as they were performed in his day in the wonderful reconstruction of The Globe on the south bank of the Thames near Southwark Bridge. A ghostly actress may still be acting out her role in one of his plays at the Old Vic Theatre in Lambeth, on the corner of The Cut and Waterloo Road (SE1), which was famous for its productions of Shakespeare's plays in the early 20th century. In their book 'Haunted West End Theatres' (2007), the authors Ian John Shillito and Becky Walsh report a number of accounts by members of staff who worked at the theatre over the years, who described seeing the spectral lady move away in front of them before disappearing through a solid wall. The phantom lady is dressed in period costume and appears to be in some distress, frantically wringing her bloody hands. One theory is that she is the spectre of a Shakespearian actress of the past who is reprising her role as Lady Macbeth, re-enacting the famous sleepwalking scene after Duncan's murder when she desperately tries to wash his blood from her hands: "Out, damned spot! out, I say!".

From the Old Vic, we now follow Waterloo Road (the A301) from Lambeth and Southwark as it crosses the river over Waterloo Bridge to the north bank. The present bridge, seen in the view on the opposite page with the Festival Pier and Southbank Centre on the right-hand side, was built between 1939 and 1945, during the Second World War, and was nicknamed the 'Ladies' Bridge' because it was constructed by a largely female labour force. It replaced the original bridge which had opened in 1817 as a memorial to the Battle of Waterloo of 1815 in which the Allied forces defeated Napoleon Bonaparte's army and put an end to the Napoleonic wars. Arches of the old Waterloo Bridge (demolished in 1936) can be seen on the right of the photograph on page 23.

The old Waterloo Bridge was said to be haunted by the terrifying spectre of a headless man following the discovery of a carpetbag containing the dismembered remains of a human body near one of its abutments in 1857; the gruesome find was made by two Thames lightermen rowing out to a barge in the river. When a police surgeon pieced together what was left of the dismembered body he found that its head, hands and feet were missing, and that the unfortunate victim had been stabbed nine times. The body was never identified, and the mystery of who the man was has never been resolved. At the time the body was discovered, it was thought most likely that the murdered man was a foreign sailor from one of the ships anchored in the Thames. A different and much darker theory was held by Sir Robert Anderson (1841-1918), who served as the second Assistant Commissioner (Crime) of the London Metropolitan Police from 1888 to 1901 and was also an intelligence officer. In 1910 he published his memoirs, 'The Lighter Side of My Official Life', in which he stated his belief that the victim was an undercover agent of the Italian Police who had been sent to London to infiltrate a group of Italian revolutionaries based in Soho, and was murdered by them after his cover was blown. Having mutilated his corpse so he could not be identified, they then disposed of his remains in the river.

LONDON, WATERLOO BRIDGE 2003 L1305705

If Sir Robert was correct in his theory, then this is not the only link between Waterloo Bridge and the murky world of secret agents and mysterious murders. In 1969 a dissident writer called Georgi Markov defected from Communist Bulgaria to Britain where he worked as a broadcaster and journalist for the BBC World Service and other European radio stations, using those forums to conduct a campaign of criticism against the Bulgarian regime. In September 1978, whilst waiting at a bus stop on Waterloo Bridge, Mr Markov felt a sharp jab in his leg. He looked behind him and saw a man picking up an umbrella from the ground. Soon afterwards Mr Markov complained of feeling unwell, and three days later he was dead. It was later established that he had been injected with a small pellet containing ricin, a deadly poison, probably by an agent of the Bulgarian secret services using the specially adapted umbrella as a weapon. There have been no tales – so far – that Mr Markov's spirit haunts the bridge, but who knows what might be told in the future, as this tragic event becomes part of the folklore of London?

The photograph on the opposite page shows the Victoria Embankment on the north bank of the Thames, with arches of the old Waterloo Bridge on the right-hand side. Prominent in this view is 'Cleopatra's Needle', an enormous Egyptian obelisk dating from 1,500BC which was given to Britain in 1819 by the Viceroy of Egypt in commemoration of the British victories against the French of the Battle of the Nile in 1798 and the Battle of Alexandria in 1801, during the Napoleonic Wars; however, it remained in Egypt until 1877, when it survived an eventful sea voyage to London during which six sailors were drowned. The obelisk was erected on the Victoria Embankment in 1878, and the names of the sailors who perished on its journey are recorded on a bronze plaque attached to the foot of its mounting stone. Some people think that the ghosts of those drowned sailors may be responsible for the sounds of groans, wailing and eerie mocking laughter that have been heard around the obelisk at night by those with ears to listen…

The area of the Victoria Embankment around Waterloo Bridge and Cleopatra's Needle is purportedly a very haunted part of London, possibly because over the years it seems to have exerted an almost magnetic pull on the depressed and despairing, and has a sad reputation for the number of suicide attempts that have taken place there. This was famously commemorated in Thomas Hood's poignant poem of 1844, 'The Bridge of Sighs', about a homeless and despairing young woman who had been forced into prostitution, who ended her life by throwing herself into the Thames from the old Waterloo Bridge. One of the most famous spectres said to haunt this area at night is a tall, naked figure that startles passers-by when it runs from the shadows and leaps over the wall into the river and then mysteriously disappears, but there is never any sound of a splash, or a ripple left on the water…

**LONDON, VICTORIA EMBANKMENT
AND CLEOPATRA'S NEEDLE c1890** L130189a

The imposing building seen on the right in the background of the photograph on the previous page is the river frontage of Somerset House, whose main facade faces The Strand just east of Waterloo Bridge. The central block of this magnificent Neoclassical building dates from 1776–96, and was built on the site of an earlier Tudor mansion to house a variety of public offices, including the Navy Office. A

regular visitor to the Admiralty and Navy Board at Somerset House in those days would have been Britain's naval hero of the Napoleonic Wars, Vice-Admiral Lord Nelson (1758-1805), whose brother Maurice also worked there. Located in the South Wing of the building is one of the most remarkable staircases in London, now known as the Nelson Stair although it was originally called the Navy Staircase. This handsome rotunda structure winds sinuously up through the building with stairs and landings attached to the wall, with an unusual combination of curves and straight sections. The present Nelson Stair is not the original staircase of Somerset House, as that was destroyed during an air-raid in the Second World War, but it was rebuilt as an exact copy. Lord Nelson is known to have climbed the original staircase for a meeting with Sir Andrew Snape Hamond, Comptroller of the Navy, in 1805, prior to setting sail on his last voyage, which ended in his naval triumph against a combined French and Spanish fleet at the Battle of Trafalgar off the coast of Spain near Cadiz, but in which he was fatally wounded. His body was brought back to London to be given a state funeral in St Paul's Cathedral, where it rests in a magnificent tomb in the crypt.

LONDON, TRAFALGAR SQUARE c1960 L1305091

Lord Nelson's greatest naval victory is commemorated in London in the name of Trafalgar Square, created in the 1830s. The centrepiece of the square is Nelson's Column, 52 metres (170 feet) high, which is topped off with a massive statue of the great man. You might expect Lord Nelson's spirit to roam this grand public space that honours him, but it seems his ghost prefers to wander the precincts of Somerset House that are more familiar to him from his earthly life, and where a portrait of him graces the Seamen's Waiting Hall in the Embankment building. Sightings of his pale wraith have been reported there on bright mornings, where his shimmering ghost walks briskly across the courtyard of Somerset House towards the part that used to be the Admiralty Office. As in his earthly life, the spectre of Lord Nelson appears frail and thin, with an empty jacket sleeve hanging to one side – Nelson lost his right arm at the Battle of Tenerife in 1797 – and some witnesses have described a misty, vapourish cloud hovering above his head. The ghostly figure is usually seen from a distance, and vanishes away if approached.

LONDON, THE HOUSES OF PARLIAMENT 1908 L130149

One of London's most iconic buildings is the Palace of Westminster, better known as the Houses of Parliament, which stands on the north bank of the Thames. A famous feature of the building is its massive clock tower. The name 'Big Ben' is often used to describe the clock tower together with its clock and bell, but this is actually just the nickname of the Great Bell of the tower, which sounds the hour. The Palace of Westminster does not – so far – seem to have any ghost stories associated with it, despite its Gothic appearance, but there is a tradition that 'Big Ben' has a spooky effect on something over the river…

On the opposite bank of the Thames a short distance upriver from the Houses of Parliament is Lambeth Palace, which is the official residence of the Archbishop of Canterbury, the head of the Church of England. Beside the palace is the redundant church of St-Mary-at-Lambeth, which now houses the Museum of Garden History. In its churchyard is an ornately carved stone tomb that holds the remains of five members of the Tradescant family, including the two John Tradescants, father and son, who were famous gardeners, botanists and plant collectors of the 17th century. John Tradescant the Elder (c1570s-1638) introduced many plants and flowers into this country that are part of the modern gardener's repertory, including the genus of flowering plants named 'Tradescantia' after him. His son, John Tradescant the Younger (1608-1662) visited Virginia in America to collect plants, and amongst the trees he introduced to Britain were magnolias, as well as garden plants such as phlox and asters. The sides of the tomb are decorated with carvings representing the Tradescants' collection of plants and curios from around the world, whilst a poem carved on its lid describes how the two gardeners

'Transplanted now themselves, sleep here, and when
Angels shall with their trumpets waken men
And fire shall purge the world, these hence shall rise
And change this garden for a Paradise.'

There is a local legend in Lambeth that a ghost will appear if you dance around the Tradescant tomb twelve times whilst Big Ben across the river strikes midnight!

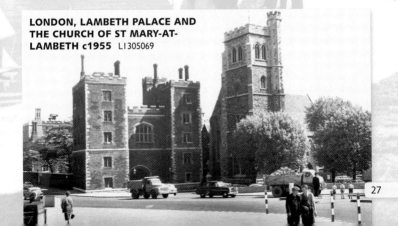

LONDON, LAMBETH PALACE AND THE CHURCH OF ST MARY-AT-LAMBETH c1955 L1305069

LONDON, WESTMINSTER ABBEY 1908 L130150

Just west of the Houses of Parliament is Westminster Abbey. The correct name for Westminster Abbey is the Collegiate Church of St Peter, but in the 11th century it became known as 'west minster' to distinguish it from the nearby 'east minster' of St Paul's Cathedral. This sublime abbey is one of Britain's most famous religious buildings. In the 13th century Henry III (1207-1272) began the reshaping of Edward the Confessor's old church, rebuilding it in French Gothic style, and restyling continued until well into the 16th century.

Westminster Abbey is the final resting place of many famous people, including Elizabeth I (1558-1603) and Mary, Queen of Scots, who was executed by order of Elizabeth I in 1587. The area known as 'Poets Corner' in the south transept is the burial place of illustrious writers, playwrights and poets, many famous musicians are buried in the 'Musicians Aisle' (the north choir aisle), and the Statesmen's Aisle in the north transept is where a number of great names from British history lie at peace. However, one of the most poignant tombs in the abbey is that of the Unknown Warrior, marked with a black marble slab in the nave, which commemorates all the soldiers who died in the First World War (1914-18) who have no other memorial or known grave because their remains were never found or could not be identified. On 11th November 1920 (Armistice Day), the body of an unknown soldier who had died in the war was given a state funeral here, buried in Westminster Abbey 'among the kings' in soil brought from the battlefields of France. The sad figure of a ghostly soldier is said to materialise beside the grave from time to time, after the crowds of tourists have left this hallowed building and all is quiet. Witnesses have described him as wearing the mud-stained khaki uniform of a First World War infantryman, although he does not wear a helmet or cap. He stands for a moment of quiet contemplation beside the tomb with his head bowed, and then vanishes away into thin air. Is he the spirit of the unknown warrior who was buried there? Or is this a ghost of one of the hundreds of thousands of brave men who died in that dreadful conflict, sadly paying homage to their sacrifice?

LONDON, WESTMINSTER ABBEY, THE TOMB OF THE UNKNOWN WARRIOR c1965 L1305260

LONDON, WESTMINSTER ABBEY, THE CLOISTERS c1900 L130228

The most famous ghost said to roam Westminster Abbey is a
phantom monk known as 'Father Benedictus', who haunts the
cloisters. His tall, rangy figure is dressed in the hooded black habit
of a Benedictine monk and people who have seen his shade have
described it as floating above the ground, probably because the
floor of the cloisters has been lowered since the time of his earthly
life many centuries ago. Father Benedictus is said to materialise in
the cloisters in the early evening, and is very friendly – there have
been reports of him chatting politely to visitors, some of whom did
not realise that he was only there in spectral form until he silently
vanished away into a wall! Father Benedictus is believed to be the
ghost of a murdered monk, but there are several theories about
when he died. One is that he was killed by thieves in 1303 after
interrupting them whilst they were robbing the Pyx Chamber, the
undercroft of the monks' dormitory that was used as a treasury in the
Middle Ages and is accessed from the Great Cloister. An alternative
date was put forward by a spiritualist who claimed to have made

contact with his shade in the 1930s, reporting that Father Benedictus told her he was actually murdered in the 16th century, during the reign of Henry VIII. However, there are no official records of any monks being murdered in the abbey at either period.

Another ghost said to haunt Westminster Abbey is that of John Bradshaw (1602-1654), a prominent 17th-century politician, lawyer and judge who in January 1649 was granted a lease of the deanery at Westminster Abbey; during his time there he also used a small room in the triforium to work in, at the south-west end of the abbey. It was also in January 1649, following the Civil War, that John Bradshaw was appointed President of the Court of Justice set up to try King Charles I, who was charged with treason for waging war against his own subjects. At the end of the trial Bradshaw refused to allow King Charles to speak in his own defence, pronounced the death sentence on the king, and signed the death warrant authorising his execution. Bradshaw's remorseful ghost is said to walk from the triforium every year on the anniversary of King Charles's execution on 30th January 1649 in repentance for his role in the king's death, and is believed to be responsible for the mysterious sounds of disembodied footsteps that have been heard at night in the passage and on the stairs.

On the eastern side of Whitehall, which runs from Parliament Square (behind Westminster Abbey) to Trafalgar Square, is the Banqueting House. Designed by Inigo Jones in 1622, this is the only substantial remnant of Whitehall Palace, the main residence of the English monarchs in London from 1530 until 1698 when it was destroyed by fire. It was from the Banqueting House's central window that in 1649 King Charles I stepped out onto the scaffold erected outside the building for his execution as a 'tyrant, traitor, murderer and public enemy of the Commonwealth of England'. An equestrian statue of the king now stands on a traffic island at Charing Cross, at the Trafalgar Square end of Whitehall, looking towards the spot where he met his end.

Whitehall is the traditional home of the offices of government, including the Treasury, Home Office and Privy Council. Just past the Cenotaph in Whitehall is the entrance to Downing Street, where 'Number 10' is the official residence of the Prime Minister. Dating from the late 17th century, Number 10 has been considerably extended into neighbouring houses and altered over the years; it now contains around 100 rooms used for residential, office and reception purposes, where national leaders and foreign dignitaries are met and entertained. Number 10 is reputed to be haunted by a number of ghosts, one of which is described as a man wearing clothes dating from the Regency period, which lasted from 1811 until 1820, when the Prince Regent became King George IV following the death of his father, King George III, who had spent the last years of his reign suffering from insanity. The ghostly man was seen on several occasions by workmen carrying out a programme of alterations inside Number 10 in the late 1950s and early 1960s, and was also seen in the garden, where the witness said he moved away towards the wall that backs onto Horse Guards Parade and then just disappeared. Because the spectral man is dressed in Regency fashion some people think he is the shade of Spencer Perceval, who was Prime Minister from 1809 until 1812 and the only British Prime Minister to have been assassinated. His killer was John Bellingham, whose job with a Liverpool merchant had involved him travelling to Russia where he had been jailed after contracts he negotiated had failed. On his return to England he believed he was entitled to compensation from the government for his unjust imprisonment, but this was refused. On 11th May 1812 an embittered Bellingham went to the House of Commons where he shot the Prime Minister with a pistol. Perceval's body was brought back to Number 10 Downing Street, where it lay for five days before his funeral.

If the ghostly man really is the shade of Spencer Perceval, he is not the only Prime Minister who may still reside at Number 10 in spirit form. There have been many reports by staff working there of the strong odour of cigar

SIR WINSTON CHURCHILL (1874-1965)

smoke in the rooms and corridors of the basement of the building, which some attribute to the shade of Sir Winston Churchill, Britain's inspirational Prime Minister during the dark days of the Second World War, who was famously fond of a good cigar. The basement is also said to be haunted by a ghostly little girl who sometimes holds your hand, but who she might be remains a mystery, as does the identity of 'The Lady', a rather grand woman wearing a long gown and a splendid set of pearls who is said to linger in the Pillared Drawing Room of Number 10, which nowadays is used as a venue for official functions and the formal signing of international agreements.

For security reasons the famous black front door of Number 10 Downing Street cannot be opened from the outside because it has no handle, and neither does it have a keyhole – the door is opened from the inside by staff watching on a screen. Visitors entering the building then pass through a scanner and a set of security gates manned by armed guards. However, all this high-tech security is completely ignored by the mysterious tall, smartly-dressed gentleman wearing a top hat who strides determinedly through the entrance lobby of Number 10 and then exits the building by walking straight through the closed front door!

LONDON, WHITEHALL c1910 L130646

On the left of this view of Whitehall, just past the cyclists, is the
entrance to the Old Admiralty, or Ripley Building. This is the oldest
part of Admiralty House, the home of the First Lord of the Admiralty.
A holder of that office several times in the 18th century was John
Montagu, 4th Earl of Sandwich, who lived there with his mistress,
Martha Ray. Martha had an affair with a man called James Hackman,
but refused to leave the Earl for him. In 1779, overcome with jealousy,
Hackman shot Martha dead as she was leaving a theatre in Covent
Garden. Her ghost is said to roam her former home, and amongst
those who claimed to have seen her were Sir Winston Churchill, who
lived there during two terms as First Lord of the Admiralty, from 1911
to 1915 and 1939 to 1940, and the Labour politician Denis Healey, who
occupied quarters in the building with his family after his appointment
as Secretary of State for Defence in 1964. In June 1969 several
newspapers ran the story that the Healey family had regularly seen
Martha's ghost, but Mr Healey told reporters that her presence was not
at all frightening and his children had become very fond of 'the lady'.

The Mall leads from Trafalgar Square to Buckingham Palace, the principal London home of the British monarch, seen in the background of this view before its East Front was remodelled in 1913. On its southern side is St James's Park, where the lake is said to be haunted by a headless lady in a blood-spattered dress who rises from the waters and drifts onto dry land, then runs away into the undergrowth. She also roams between the park and the Cockpit Steps, east of the Wellington Barracks on Birdcage Walk which runs along the southern edge of the park. She is thought to be the ghost of the wife of a sergeant of one of the Guards regiments who murdered her in the 1780s, decapitated her and threw her body into the canal in the park, which was later developed into the lake. Her phantom has roamed ever since, searching for its head. Buckingham Palace itself is supposed to be roamed by a ghostly monk who appears on the terrace overlooking the gardens behind the building. He is bound in heavy chains, in punishment for some transgression in his earthly life, and clanks and moans as he shuffles along the terrace for a few moments, then fades away. He only appears on Christmas Day though – no wonder members of the Royal Family prefer to spend the festive season at Sandringham House in Norfolk!

**LONDON, BUCKINGHAM PALACE
FROM ST JAMES'S PARK c1890**
L130385

Another haunted royal palace in this part of London is St James's Palace, in Pall Mall just north of St James's Park. One of London's oldest palaces, it was commissioned by Henry VIII in the 16th century and constructed in Tudor style in red brick around four courtyards. King Charles II restored the palace in the 1660s after his restoration to the throne following the Civil War, and it became the principal residence of the monarch in London in 1698, after Whitehall Palace was destroyed by fire. At this time it also became the administrative centre and 'official residence' of the monarchy, a role it still retains, although it is no longer a royal residence. As the most senior royal palace in the UK it gives its name to the Royal Court, 'the Court of St James's'.

St James's Palace is said to be roamed by the gruesome spectre of a man with his throat cut. This is believed to be the unhappy shade of Joseph Sellis, who on the night of 31st May 1810 was found dead in his room at the palace, having apparently killed himself. The palace at that time was the home of Ernest Augustus, Duke of Cumberland, a son of King George III, and Sellis was one of his valets. On the night of Sellis's death the Duke claimed that he had been attacked with his regimental sabre whilst he lay sleeping in his bed, but frightened the assailant away when he woke and called for help. When staff went to find Sellis to attend his master, they found his blood-stained, lifeless corpse in his room, with his throat cut from ear to ear. They concluded that he had been the person who attacked the Duke, and had committed suicide after failing in his attempt to kill him. However, the Duke of Cumberland was highly unpopular and had many enemies, and rumours soon spread about the reasons why Sellis might have attacked him, one theory being that the Duke was having an affair with his wife, and another that the Duke had seduced his daughter. There was also speculation that Sellis might have been murdered by the Duke to keep him quiet about something unsavoury he had found out about his master, and that the injuries the Duke had sustained were self-inflicted, part of the cover up for his crime that would give credence to his tale about an assault and explain Sellis's supposed suicide. In his book 'Wicked Ernest', about the Duke, published by Selfmark Books in 2002, John Wardroper records that in 1815 the Duke made a 'dreadful confession' to his friend and aide-de-camp Captain Charles Jones, who later recorded that the Duke told him: 'You know that miserable business of Sellis's, that wretch, I was forced to destroy him in self-defence, the villain threatened to propagate a report & I had no alternative.' The record of the Duke of Cumberland's confession to Captain Jones is now in the royal archives at Windsor Castle.

Whatever the truth about the death of the unfortunate Sellis, he was buried in accordance with the procedure for suicides at that time, at dead of night without Christian rites in unconsecrated ground at a place where three roads meet, which in his case was near what is now the Sherlock Holmes public house at the junction of Northumberland Street and Northumberland Avenue in Westminster, the road systems having changed a great deal since that time. As was also then the custom with the burials of suicides, a stake was driven through his heart to prevent his unquiet spirit wandering. That doesn't appear to have worked though – his gruesome ghost is said to roam the area around the Sherlock Holmes pub where he was buried as well as St James's Palace itself, where it not only haunts the room where he met his end but also wanders the corridors of the building, leaving the sickly stench of blood behind him.

A short distance south-east of Hyde Park Corner is one of London's most famous haunted pubs, the Grenadier in Belgravia, hidden away in Wilton Row, just behind Wilton Crescent, to the north of Belgrave Square. Wilton Row is a former mews (a row of stables) which used to be part of the barracks of the Duke of Wellington's guards – the 'Iron Duke', victor of the Battle of Waterloo in 1815, lived nearby in Apsley House at Hyde Park Corner – and the upper floor of The Grenadier was used as the officers' mess. The pub is said to be haunted by the spirit of a young subaltern who was caught cheating at cards in the mess and whose comrades flogged him severely for his dishonourable behaviour; after his beating he staggered down to what is now the cellar where he died as a result. His unhappy shade is said to have haunted the building ever since. A great deal of paranormal activity seems to occur in the pub, particularly in September, including the sound of disembodied footsteps in empty rooms, and strange moaning sounds coming from the cellar. Objects are mysteriously moved around or disappear, and tables and chairs sometimes appear to be rattled by an unseen hand…

Hyde Park is Inner London's largest public park. A feature of the park is the Serpentine, a 40-acre recreational lake that was created in the 1730s, although that is properly only the name for the eastern half of the lake; the western half is the Long Water, with the two areas divided by the Serpentine Bridge that marks the boundary between Hyde Park and Kensington Gardens. It was here that 21-year-old Harriet Westbrook Shelley met her death in December 1816. She was the first wife of the poet Percy Bysshe Shelley, who had left her for Mary Godwin who he later married. Harriet had then taken a lover who had made her pregnant and then abandoned her, and she threw herself into the Serpentine in despair. Her ghost is said to linger there still, and perhaps it was her spectral hand that two ladies saw one winter's day as they were walking in the park; it appeared to reach up from the water as if beseeching help, before sinking back into the stillness of the lake.

On the western side of Kensington Gardens is Kensington Palace, formerly Nottingham House which King William III (1650-1702) turned into his 'country residence'. King George II (1727-60) made Kensington Palace one of his principal homes and lived there for much of the year. He was the second of the Hanoverian kings, who were joint monarchs of both Britain and the Kingdom of Hanover in what is now Germany. They were descended from Charles I's daughter Elizabeth, and their line came to the throne in 1714 after Queen Anne died with no living heir. This dual kingdom arrangement only finished with the accession to the British throne of Queen Victoria in 1837. Under Salic law a female could not rule Hanover, so it passed to the nearest male heir and became separate again from Britain.

The State Rooms of Kensington Palace are open to the public, including the King's Gallery. On the wall over the fireplace of this room is a large dial featuring a painted map of north-western Europe. This is a wind-dial, which is connected to a weathervane on the roof over the main entrance to the palace, and was created for King William III so he could see which way the wind was blowing, where his navy was likely to be heading, and when the posts were likely to arrive. It is still in working order. The direction of the wind was of great importance to King George II in his final days, when the ill and aged king was desperately waiting for a ship to arrive with despatches from his beloved Hanover, where he was born and had lived for 31 years until he came to Britain in 1714, when his father ascended the throne as King George I. Sadly for the king, he died before the wind changed and the ship arrived. King George's ghost is said to haunt the palace, especially when the wind blows strongly from the west; legend says his sad face is sometimes seen gazing out of a window towards the weather-vane, and the sound of his voice with its heavy German accent can still be heard drifting through the corridors, plaintively muttering in frustration 'Vy don't zey kom?'.

Our tour now moves to Mayfair, where Number 50 Berkeley Square was famous in the 19th-century as the most haunted house in London. Something was said to lurk in a certain room on an upper floor of the house that was so horrific it had scared people to death. Its creepy reputation was discussed by W E Howlett in the 2nd August 1879 issue of the literary journal 'Notes and Queries', citing a reference that had appeared in May of that year in 'Mayfair' magazine: 'The house contains at least one room of which the atmosphere is supernaturally fatal to body and mind. A girl saw, heard and felt such horror in it that she went mad, and never recovered sanity enough to tell how or why. A gentleman, a disbeliever in ghosts, dared to sleep in number 50 and was found a corpse in the middle of the floor after frantically ringing for help in vain. Rumour suggests other cases of the same kind, all ending in death, madness, or both as a result of sleeping, or trying to sleep in that room. The very party walls of the house, when touched, are found saturated with electric horror…'

Many unsubstantiated or downright fictional stories have become associated with the house over the years, but two interesting tales were recounted by Jessie A Middleton in 'The Grey Ghost Book', published in 1912. She recorded a story she had heard many years earlier about the ghost there of a little girl who had been frightened to death by a servant in the nursery at the top of the house; her sobbing ghost, wearing a 'Scotch plaid frock', was haunting the house to such an extent that no one would live there, and it did indeed stand empty for some years in the late 19th century. Another ghost said to roam the building was of a young girl called Adeline, who fell to her death from an upper window whilst trying to escape from a lecherous uncle who was abusing her.

Since 1938 the house has been the premises of Maggs Brothers Ltd, the famous antiquarian booksellers, and has not been disturbed by any untoward paranormal activity during their occupancy. However, it still retains its reputation, and visitors often ask the staff if they have any trouble with ghosts. The answer is 'No' – at least, not so far!

A short distance north of Berkeley Square is Brook Street (W1) where what is now Number 25 was the home of the composer George Frideric Handel (1685-1759) for 36 years from 1723 until his death in 1759. The upper floors of the house were taken over by the Handel House Trust in 2000 and now form The Handel House Museum, which opened in 2001. It was widely reported in the media in 2001 that several members of staff preparing the premises for its public opening as the museum believed they had seen a ghost in the bedroom where Handel had died in 1759, and a Roman Catholic priest was called in to perform an exorcism. The Telegraph newspaper reported on the story in an article by Catherine Milner in its issue of 15th July 2001, in which Martin Egglestone, a trust fundraiser, reported seeing the ghost twice in the bedroom of the house. Mr Egglestone said of the first sighting: 'Suddenly, the air got very thick and I saw a shape, higher than me, like the imprint on the back of your retina when you close your eyes, having been looking at the sun for too long.' On the second occasion the entity was also seen by another staff member working with Mr Egglestone, who went on to make it clear that neither of them experienced any feeling of malevolence from its presence.

An interesting addition to this story is that between 1968 and 1969 the rock legend Jimi Hendrix (1942-1970) lived on the upper floor of the adjoining house to The Handel House Museum, Number 23, and claimed that he once saw the great composer's bewigged ghost disappearing into the adjoining wall of the houses.

The two properties in Brook Street are now marked by blue plaques commemorating their former occupants, both heroes of musical history although of two very different styles. Sadly, Jimi Hendrix does not seem to have returned in spirit form to visit his former home, despite being very happy during his stay there.

Theatres are notoriously haunted buildings and London's are no exception, where a number of performers from the past seem reluctant to take their final bow.

The shade of William Terris is said to haunt the Adelphi Theatre on the Strand. This matinée idol and actor-manager of the 19th century was stabbed to death outside the Maiden Lane entrance to the Adelphi in 1897 by a small-time actor jealous of his success. The story goes that Terris whispered 'I will be back' as he lay dying, and he certainly seems to have kept his word. As well as haunting the theatre, his restless ghost seems to wander along Maiden Lane where he met his end, where a mysterious man dressed in 'old-fashioned' clothes was seen by a tourist in 1928 before suddenly disappearing 'like a bubble bursting'. William Terris's shade is also said to visit Covent Garden Underground Station, probably because in his earthly life Terris was a regular customer at a baker's shop that formerly stood on the site. Sightings of his ghost at the station were reported over 40 times by a ticket inspector at the station called Jack Hayden in the 1950s, who described the apparition as a tall man in a grey suit, wearing a Homburg hat. On one occasion when he was working in his office, the door of the room began to rattle violently. When he opened the door he found himself face to face with the spectral man, who stared at him for a few seconds then turned and walked away, disappearing into thin air in front of Mr Hayden's startled gaze. Another member of staff in the 1950s, a ticket collector called Victor Locker, also reported seeing the apparition, which he described as a terrifying, rather threatening force. Mr Hayden and Mr Locker both immediately identified the phantom man as William Terris when they were shown a picture of him.

One of the city's best-known theatres is the London Palladium in Argyll Street, off Oxford Street. A spectral lady dressed in a crinoline gown is said to roam the building, particularly around the Crimson Staircase that leads up to the Royal Circle; she has been seen gliding up and down the staircase many times by staff members as well as theatrical performers in shows at the Palladium. No one is sure who she was in her earthly life, but perhaps she is linked with Argyll House, the former home of the Dukes of Argyll, which stood on the site of the theatre until it was demolished in 1860.

Two haunted theatres face each other across the road in Haymarket, which runs between Piccadilly and Pall Mall. On one side is the Theatre Royal, Haymarket (or Haymarket Theatre), which is roamed by the friendly ghost of the actor, playwright and comedian John Buckstone (1802-1879), who managed the theatre from 1853 to 1877. He usually manifests in Dressing Room 1, his favourite dressing room during his earthly career treading the boards, where drawers and wardrobe doors open and close by themselves and disembodied footsteps have been heard walking around the room, but he has also been glimpsed around the theatre's corridors and stairwells, dressed in a long tailcoat of 19th-century fashion. Famous stars who have claimed to have seen him include Margaret Rutherford, Sir Donald Sinden and Dame Judi Dench. On the other side of the road is Her Majesty's Theatre (its name changes from His or Her Majesty's Theatre according to the sex of the current monarch), which was built in the 1890s for the actor-manager Sir Herbert Beerbohm Tree (1852-1917). He may still visit the theatre in spirit form to watch performances from the top box, stage right, which was his favourite seat in the house in his earthly life. Theatregoers who use the box sometimes experience sudden drops in temperature, and the door to the box has been seen mysteriously opening on its own accord – or being opened by an unseen hand as Sir Herbert lets himself in?

London's oldest working theatre is the Theatre Royal, Drury Lane in Covent Garden, commonly known as just 'Drury Lane'. The present theatre building is the fourth theatre to have stood on this site. The first Theatre Royal was built in 1663, under a Royal Patent from King Charles II, hence its name, and the king's orange-seller-turned-actress mistress Nell Gwynn performed there. The third theatre, built in 1794, was burnt down in 1809. The present building opened in 1812 and is probably the most haunted theatre in London. Many ghosts are said to roam the theatre – here are some of the most famous:

In 1735 the actor Charles Macklin caused the death of a fellow thespian, Thomas Hallam, in the Green Room of an earlier theatre building. The two men were having a violent argument about a trivial subject – which of them had the right to wear a particular wig. 'God damn you for a blackguard, scrub, rascal!' shouted Macklin, who was notorious for his volatile nature and uncontrollable temper, and he thrust his walking stick into Hallam's face. It pierced his eye, and the unfortunate man later died as a result of the injury. Macklin

CHARLES MACKLIN
(1669-1797)

was prosecuted for the incident but never sentenced. He went on to live a very long life, dying in 1797, but his ghost seems to have returned to haunt the theatre in remorse for causing Hallam's death. His tall, grim-faced phantom is said to wander the area in front of what used to be the pit of the theatre, appearing most often in the early evening, shortly before a performance begins.

The most famous ghost of the Theatre Royal, Drury Lane is the mysterious Man in Grey, an apparition of a young man dressed in 18th-century fashion – he wears a powdered wig, a long grey cloak over a ruffled shirt and leather riding boots, and either wears or carries a tricorn hat. He appears during daylight hours, between 9am and 6pm, and has been seen by countless staff and performers at the theatre, as well audience members during matinée performances, although he fades away if he is approached or someone tries to talk to him. He follows a specific route as he moves around the theatre – after occupying a particular seat in the fourth row of the upper circle, he moves across the theatre along the gangway at the back; finally he vanishes away at the far end of the theatre, disappearing through the wall on the Russell Street side of the building. No one knows who he is or why he haunts the theatre, but he is surely linked to the gruesome discovery made by workmen carrying out alterations to the theatre in the mid 19th century. They noticed that a part of the wall on one side of the upper circle sounded hollow – precisely the spot where the ghost disappears. When they broke through the wall they discovered a secret bricked-up chamber that contained the skeleton of a man with a dagger protruding from his ribcage. The skeleton of the murdered man must have been hidden there at some time before 1796, for the wall had been left untouched during earlier rebuilding work at that date. His remains were given a respectful burial in a graveyard at the corner of Russell Street and Drury Lane, which was later deconsecrated and is now a small open space called Drury Lane Gardens. His identity will never be known now, but if the Man in Grey is indeed his spectre, the staff and performers do not find his presence threatening or malevolent – in fact, they welcome his visits as the appearance of his ghost at the beginning of a new production at the theatre is always a sign it will be a great success. One of his favourite shows in recent years must have been the long-running musical 'Miss Saigon' – not only did he appear when it first began, he also manifested whenever there was a change of cast!

The ghost of Joseph Grimaldi (1778-1837) is also said to haunt the Theatre Royal, Drury Lane where he was a regular performer, particularly in pantomime. A comic superstar of his times and famous in theatre and circus history as the father of modern clowning, he invented the white-faced clown character that is known as Joey after him. The highly physical nature of his performances took their toll on his body, and when he gave his last public performance at the Theatre Royal on 28th June 1828 he was no longer able to stand; he had to be carried on to the stage and gave his performance seated in a chair, but he still had the audience roaring with laughter and the show was a triumphant end to a wonderful career. Grimaldi died in 1837 and was buried in St James's churchyard on Pentonville Road in Islington in north London. The churchyard was later deconsecrated, and the part that includes Grimaldi's grave is now Joseph Grimaldi Park, a short distance east of King's Cross Station. In typical clown fashion, Grimaldi's playful spirit at the Theatre Royal is said to administer mischievous kicks with its spectral foot to the derrières of staff and performers as they go about their tasks. The rather startling sight of his disembodied head with its face painted white in his distinctive clown make-up is also said to float around the theatre or hover at the back of one of its boxes, happily watching the performance on the stage – the reason why just his head appears is that Grimaldi was terrified of being buried alive and left instructions that he should be decapitated after his death, to make completely sure he was dead!

Is it the ghost of the Man in Grey that is responsible for the invisible 'helping hands' that a number of performers at the Theatre Royal have felt on their shoulders or back, pushing and guiding them into positions on the stage from where they can best deliver their lines or songs? Or is it Grimaldi's spirit, or perhaps the friendly, helpful shade of another unidentified but highly skilled theatrical performer from the past that lingers on the stage to help inexperienced young performers? No one knows, but the 'helpful hands' at the Theatre Royal, Drury Lane have become part of the legend of this fascinating building.

A famous chronicler of 19th-century London was the author Charles Dickens (1812-1870). He lived in several houses in London during his life, but the only one to have survived is 48 Doughty Street, in the London Borough of Camden (WC1), where he lived from March 1837 until December 1839. It is now open to the public as The Charles Dickens Museum. According to Richard Jones in his book 'Haunted London' (New Holland, 2008), Dickens often returns to his former home

CHARLES DICKENS

in spirit form – a former curator of the house claimed that during her time there she frequently saw the 'distinctive figure' of his ghost 'bounding enthusiastically along the hallway and up the staircase'.

One of the most notorious and feared places in London in the past was Newgate Prison, whose 'dreadful walls had hidden so much misery and such unspeakable anguish', as Charles Dickens wrote in his novel 'Oliver Twist'. In 1783 London's gallows were moved to Newgate from the former execution site at Tyburn, and executions took place in public in the open space in front of the prison from then until 1868, after which they were carried out within the prison walls, away from public gaze. Executions following judicial death sentences continued to take place inside Newgate Prison until 1902, when both the prison and the court that stood next to it were demolished. The Central Criminal Court, more commonly known as the Old Bailey, now stands on the prison's former site in central London, just west of St Paul's Cathedral. The fearsome bulk of Newgate Prison was the subject of many chilling tales of hauntings and paranormal activity whilst it stood, and one ghost from its past may still linger in the Old Bailey, where the apparition of a black-cloaked man is said to appear in response to miscarriages of justice. He is believed to be the ghost of someone who was wrongly accused of being a highwayman, sentenced to death and hanged for a crime of which he was completely innocent.

One of the most famous landmarks of London's skyline is the great dome of St Paul's Cathedral, perched on the summit of Ludgate Hill. The original medieval St Paul's Cathedral was destroyed in the Great Fire of London of 1666, and its replacement that we see today was designed by Sir Christopher Wren (1632-1723). On the wall above his grave in the south aisle at the east end of the Crypt is inscribed: 'Lector, si monumentum requiris, circumspice' – 'Reader, if you seek his monument, look around you'.

Many famous men and women have been laid to rest in this special place of worship, yet its resident ghost is said to be of a humble clergyman affectionately known as 'Whistler'. He is described as an elderly man with long grey hair who wears old-fashioned clerical robes, presumably the shade of an unidentified official of the cathedral from the past. He is reputed to haunt the Chapel of All Souls (also known as the Kitchener Memorial Chapel) on the ground floor of the north-west tower of the frontage of the cathedral – the tower on the left-hand side of the photograph on the opposite page. His appearance is always heralded by a sudden drop in temperature, then the spectral clergyman appears and glides across the chapel before disappearing into the wall to the right of its gates, whistling a low, mournful tune to himself all the while. Following the First World War of 1914 to 1918, the Chapel of All Souls was renovated in the 1920s and rededicated as a memorial chapel to Field Marshall Lord Kitchener (1850-1916) who had died at sea during the war and whose body was not recovered, and all the servicemen who had died in the conflict. During the renovation work a small door was discovered concealed in the wall at the exact spot where Whistler always disappears, behind which is a small spiral staircase winding upwards into the main fabric of the body of the cathedral. The existence as well as the purpose of both the door and the hidden staircase had been long forgotten – except by Whistler…

OPPOSITE PAGE: LONDON, ST PAUL'S CATHEDRAL c1965 L1305299

The 'City of London' is the name for a small area of central London which is the historic core around which the modern metropolis grew. The UK's banking and financial services have historically been based there and it is the home of the Bank of England in Threadneedle Street, on the left of this view, which has been much extended and rebuilt since it was first established on this site in 1734 and now covers nearly four acres. The Bank of England has been known as 'The Old Lady of Threadneedle Street' since 1797, when a political cartoon appeared depicting the Prime Minister of the Day, William Pitt the Younger, pretending to woo the Bank, personified by an elderly lady wearing a dress made of £1 notes sitting on a chest of gold. The cartoon was titled 'Political Ravishment or The Old Lady of Threadneedle Street in Danger', and the nickname stuck. However, a ghostly 'Old Lady' is also associated with the Bank of England, who regularly visits the charming garden that lies deep within the precincts of its central block as she searches for a long-lost loved one.

The apparition is dressed in full mourning attire of long black clothes and a dark veil that hides her face, causing the Bank employees to call her the 'Black Nun'. The story goes that she is the ghost of Sarah Whitehead whose brother Philip worked as a cashier at the Bank in the early 19th century. He got into debt trying to fund a lifestyle for himself and his sister that was far beyond his means and fell into bad company, consorting with fraudsters and other disreputable companions. His financial problems worsened after his dubious activities caused the Bank to ask him to resign, and he forged some cheques. His crime was discovered, and in November 1811 he was tried for forgery at the Old Bailey, found guilty and hanged a few weeks later. His friends managed to keep the news of his crime and subsequent fate from Sarah, but eventually she became puzzled by his long absence and went to the Bank to enquire about him – Philip had not told her he had lost his post there. She was then told the whole story, and the shock and grief sent Sarah out of her wits.

Her disordered mind refused to accept what had happened and every day for the rest of her long life she came to the Bank to ask if Philip had come to work yet; she was always politely told: 'Not today, madam.' The Bank employees were sympathetic towards Sarah and helped her with small gifts of money, even paying for her lodgings. Sarah died in her early sixties and was buried in the graveyard of the now demolished church of St Christopher-le-Stocks which stood near the Bank. The graveyard later became the Bank's garden, and several Bank employees have reported seeing her ghost aimlessly wandering the garden paths, still searching for her errant but beloved brother. Sarah's spectral black-shrouded figure is also said to roam outside the Bank in Threadneedle Street, asking passers-by 'Have you seen my brother?' before slowly fading away.

LONDON, THE BANK OF ENGLAND AND THE ROYAL EXCHANGE c1910   L130193

Further Reading and Acknowledgements

London is full of haunted places and ghost stories, and only a short selection could be included in this small book. For more information and further reading, the following books and website are highly recommended. They were also invaluable source material in preparing this book.

Abbott, Geoffrey: 'Ghosts of the Tower of London', Heinemann, 1980

Brandon, David & Brooke, Alan: 'Haunted London Underground', History Press, 2008

Clark, James: 'Haunted London', Tempus 2007

Coxe, Antony D Hippisley: 'Haunted Britain', Hutchinson & Co, 1973

Hallam, Jack: 'Ghosts of London', Mosby-Wolfe, 1975

Jones, Richard: 'Walking Haunted London', New Holland, 1999

Jones, Richard: 'Haunted London', New Holland, 2008

Middleton, Jessie Adelaide: 'The Grey Ghost Book', Eveleigh Nash, 1912

Price, Harry: 'Poltergeist Over England: Three Centuries of Mischievous Ghosts', David & Charles, 2012

Reader's Digest: 'Folklore, Myths and Legends of Britain', Reader's Digest Association Ltd, 1977

Shillito, Ian John & Walsh, Becky: 'Haunted West End Theatres', Tempus, 2007

Underwood, Peter: 'Haunted London', Amberley, 2010

Wardroper, John: 'Wicked Ernest', Selfmark Books, 2002

Weir, Alison: 'The Lady in the Tower – The Fall of Anne Boleyn', Jonathan Cape, 2009 (Includes an examination of the ghost stories associated with Anne Boleyn at the Tower of London)

www.hrp.org.uk – the official Historic Royal Palaces website, with information and history about the Tower of London, Hampton Court Palace, the Banqueting House in Whitehall, Kensington Palace and Kew Palace – and a few ghost stories as well!

OPPOSITE: LONDON, CLERKENWELL, PETER'S LANE c1880 L130096

FRANCIS FRITH

Francis Frith, founder of the world-famous photographic archive, was a complex and multi-talented man. A devout Quaker and a highly successful Victorian businessman, he was philosophical by nature and pioneering in outlook. By 1855 he had already established a wholesale grocery business in Liverpool, and sold it for the astonishing sum of £200,000, which is the equivalent today of over £15,000,000. Now in his thirties, and captivated by the new science of photography, Frith set out on a series of pioneering journeys up the Nile and to the Near East.

INTRIGUE AND EXPLORATION

He was the first photographer to venture beyond the sixth cataract of the Nile. Africa was still the mysterious 'Dark Continent', and Stanley and Livingstone's historic meeting was a decade into the future. The conditions for picture taking confound belief. He laboured for hours in his wicker dark-room in the sweltering heat of the desert, while the volatile chemicals fizzed dangerously in their trays. Back in London he exhibited his photographs and was 'rapturously cheered' by members of the Royal Society. His reputation as a photographer was made overnight.

VENTURE OF A LIFE-TIME

By the 1870s the railways had threaded their way across the country, and Bank Holidays and half-day Saturdays had been made obligatory by Act of Parliament. All of a sudden the working man and his family were able to enjoy days out, take holidays, and see a little more of the world.

With typical business acumen, Francis Frith foresaw that these new tourists would enjoy having souvenirs to commemorate their days out. For the next thirty years he travelled the country by train and by pony and trap, producing fine photographs of seaside resorts and beauty spots that were keenly bought by millions of Victorians. These prints were painstakingly pasted into family albums and pored over during the dark nights of winter, rekindling precious memories of summer excursions. Frith's studio was soon supplying retail shops all over the country, and by 1890 F Frith & Co had become the greatest specialist photographic publishing company in the world, with over 2,000 sales outlets, and pioneered the picture postcard.

FRANCIS FRITH'S LEGACY

Francis Frith had died in 1898 at his villa in Cannes, his great project still growing. By 1970 the archive he created contained over a third of a million pictures showing 7,000 British towns and villages.

Frith's legacy to us today is of immense significance and value, for the magnificent archive of evocative photographs he created provides a unique record of change in the cities, towns and villages throughout Britain over a century and more. Frith and his fellow studio photographers revisited locations many times down the years to update their views, compiling for us an enthralling and colourful pageant of British life and character.

We are fortunate that Frith was dedicated to recording the minutiae of everyday life. For it is this sheer wealth of visual data, the painstaking chronicle of changes in dress, transport, street layouts, buildings, housing and landscape that captivates us so much today, offering us a powerful link with the past and with the lives of our ancestors.

Computers have now made it possible for Frith's many thousands of images to be accessed almost instantly. The archive offers every one of us an opportunity to examine the places where we and our families have lived and worked down the years. Its images, depicting our shared past, are now bringing pleasure and enlightenment to millions around the world a century and more after his death.

For further information visit: www.francisfrith.com

INTERIOR DECORATION

Frith's photographs can be seen framed and as giant wall murals in thousands of pubs, restaurants, hotels, banks, retail stores and other public buildings throughout Britain. These provide interesting and attractive décor, generating strong local interest and acting as a powerful reminder of gentler days in our increasingly busy and frenetic world.

FRITH PRODUCTS

All Frith photographs are available as prints and posters in a variety of different sizes and styles. In the UK we also offer a range of other gift and stationery products illustrated with Frith photographs, although many of these are not available for delivery outside the UK – see our web site for more information on the products available for delivery in your country.

THE INTERNET

Over 100,000 photographs of Britain can be viewed and purchased on the Frith web site. The web site also includes memories and reminiscences contributed by our customers, who have personal knowledge of localities and of the people and properties depicted in Frith photographs. If you wish to learn more about a specific town or village you may find these reminiscences fascinating to browse. Why not add your own comments if you think they would be of interest to others? See **www.francisfrith.com**

PLEASE HELP US BRING FRITH'S PHOTOGRAPHS TO LIFE

Our authors do their best to recount the history of the places they write about. They give insights into how particular towns and villages developed, they describe the architecture of streets and buildings, and they discuss the lives of famous people who lived there. But however knowledgeable our authors are, the story they tell is necessarily incomplete.